DIE WITH ME

Surrendering to Suffering

Poetry by

HUNNI BLOOM

COPYRIGHT

ISBN: 979-8-9853119-5-2 (eBook)
ISBN: 979-8-9853119-3-8 (paperback)
ISBN: 979-8-9853119-4-5 (hard cover)

Cover and back design by Esther Rai.

Published by Hunni Bloom LLC, Arcola, Illinois.

www.hunnibloom.com
@hunni_bloom

for Tabby

Fold over
the hushing,
lie into the void
and maybe
just touch
the edges
of this open space.

CONTENTS

INTRODUCTION

This collection of poetry is about feeling hard, yet temporary, truths. It captures moments of deep pain, loss, and coping with trauma and suffering. It speaks to labels and diagnoses and illustrates working through difficult mental health disorders like depression, anxiety, eating disorders, post-traumatic stress, and addiction. It lays bare difficult emotions that are socially unsanctioned and taboo to express or display. It merges the internal and external worlds. All the while, woven throughout the collection, are poems that inject temporary moments of welcomed respite, as is with life. We all need moments that remind and ground us within the impermanence of life, including all of its joys *and* woes.

I wrote this collection during a period spanning nearly a year that encompassed a time of inner searching and of learning to surrender to the abundance of loss, grief, and reconciliation that my life was full of at the time. This poetry collection is a written record of my own process of surrendering to and overcoming suffering. A month prior to starting this collection, I had lost the most precious soul I had ever known, my dog of 15 years, Tabby.

I found Tabby when I was 17 years old, at a small park in my hometown of Bristol, Virginia. I used to go to this park often as a girl and throughout my teenage years. I found myself there mostly when I was angry, sad (and skipping school), but also when I was being mischievous and frolicking around with my three childhood best friends. I grew up in this park; it changed me in many ways.

One hot August afternoon, two of my friends and I were there for a late summer cross country practice. As practice for the day ended and we found our way to our cars in the parking lot, we found Tabby there. She was a puppy, looked to be less than a year old, and appeared sickly and a bit feral even. She was starving to death and was aggressive. She was all alone. It was obvious she had been both abused and was abandoned at this park and had been there for a while (several months, it seemed). One of my friends quickly drove up the street to a store to buy a can of wet dog food while us other two stayed there watching and trying to comfort her. Once the food was out and she was lured close to us, she let me pick her up; she let me hold her.

She was instantly mine, and I hers. She was my soul mate and her and I both knew it from the start. We were kindred spirits. I was a lost, hurt, angry, traumatized teenage girl who needed solace, needed shelter. Tabby became that sanctuary for me. Before Tabby, I hated animals. We had another dog at home, a golden retriever named Zeke, that I was predictably avoidant of and annoyed by. My heart was too hardened and shielded to open to love and affection from anyone, even animals. Until Tabby. Tabby and I rescued each other. She helped me survive my remaining time living at home before I was old enough to move out and be on my own.

And then when I moved out, I left her there. I had started college and lacked any capacity to care for another living thing. I left her there for many years and though she was still my girl, her and my mother developed a strong bond in my absence. She became my mother's dog, too, and more than that, she became the link that helped hold the relationship between my mother and I together.

Then, when I was 25 years old, living alone in Denver, Colorado, amidst a PhD program, my mom sent Tabby to live with me. It was a huge sacrifice of my mother, who was often lost in her own depression and despair, to let go of Tabby. It was an act of love that chiseled a deep crack through my own hardened heart. And as it began to crack, Tabby was there. Tabby and I lived together in a tiny little apartment in Denver, Colorado for three years. It was the first time I lived more than a 30-minute drive away from my parents and my siblings and it was the start of my long, arduous healing journey.

There's been much to heal from on this journey, and I am sure the journey will never aggregate; it will never completely end. Much like how a healed up broken knee often aches before a rainstorm, my mended heart will never cease to jolt with reminders of persons, places, smells, sounds, and things that hold truths of deep pain and suffering. That is both the gift and the curse of living.

And it's our soul mates that help us most along this journey. Tabby was one of my most precious and profound soul mates. During the years in Colorado, as I began cracking open and started my work of identifying, naming, and processing my own childhood and adolescent traumas, Tabby was there. More nights than I can count I laid shattered open on our living room floor, uncontrollably sobbing, Tabby nuzzled her warm snout right into my neck. She offered me comfort that I am confident saved my life, more than once. She gave me reason to walk outside of my apartment front door when I felt paralyzed and locked into my couch. She buffered interactions and relationships. She made me laugh and brought me unconditional joy. And more than once, she gave me reason to not just give up. She led me out of many dark places.

Once I finished my graduate program, Tabby and I made a new start in the Midwest. We continued our journey of healing together, in a place where "you can throw seeds anywhere any they will grow" (something my midwestern best friend from my PhD program once told me). Tabby and I began our rooting in the Midwest; we planted many of seeds. We did yoga and we danced, a lot. We taught ourselves to cook, and we spent more time enjoying the art of stillness. We spent almost four years together in the wide-open prairie.

Then, during her last year of life, Tabby developed Canine Cognitive Degeneration. She got dementia and she started dying. In a beautiful orchestration of karma, it was my mother that first noticed and pointed it out. "I don't think Tabby remembers me," she shared during Christmas when Tabby and I were home visiting. After I scoured the research, I realized that very night that Tabby had the disease. She met the diagnostic criteria of symptoms. Her behavior had turned odd: she would "get stuck" in strange places, under tables, between the recycling bin and the counter, and behind the toilet. She sometimes would just stand in front of the wall, a few inches away from it, and blankly stare. She went to the wrong side of the door opening to be let back inside. She had accidents in the house more and more frequently. When she was awake, she walked in circles a lot. She started snarling her teeth at anyone except for me (and our boyfriend, Ryan), who would get near her.

It took only six months from the Christmas I realized she had the disease to the time I had to have her euthanized. It was the hardest decision I have ever made in my life. I was angry at Tabby many times leading up to the decision. I wanted her to just go naturally, so I didn't have to make the choice to end her life. I didn't want to have to choose. I felt like she was forcing me to have to make a choice to kill her.

I also realized how much of a gift it was to have the choice. Another part of me crumbled at the thought of her passing on her own, because I wanted her to be in my arms when she left this Earth. I wanted the last thing she ever felt to be the same warmth, comfort, and indescribable love she had given me for so many years. And I knew what she was doing, that wise old soul companion of mine. She knew what she represented to me, what she was symbolic of.

She was a survivor. She had been abused as a baby and she had been abandoned and she had crossed through pain and suffering no creature should have to endure. She knew I had too. She knew the shelter and sanctuary she was for me. She knew I was a survivor too. But she knew I had more to learn. And she knew I was ready to learn how to survive on my own, without her and what she represented for me. The childhood that shackled me still needed to be released and let go of. I needed to face and heal those parts of me. It was a choice I had yet to make, a choice I had yet to identify, name, and process.

Tabby knew that if I chose to let her go, I would choose to let all that go, too. I would choose to let go of that part of myself that had to survive the abuse, trauma, and suffering that was part of my past. With her death, Tabby invited me to die with her. She summoned me to open myself up and "move and shake" the stagnant, pent-up anger, rage, sadness, fear, and loss inside of me. She helped me set myself free.

We ritualized our last three days together on Earth. I took her down to the river and we waded by the shore. Sometimes the rapids would catch her tiny, fragile little body and she would calmly and gleefully float away while I would quickly swim over to rescue her.

She told me the rescuing was done. I must learn to let her float away.

I fed her steak for every meal for three days straight–steak and green beans, her favorite vegetable. I made a circle in our yoga room with candles and incense, and I danced around and told her all the things I was grateful for of her. We had an energy reading together and it was foretold that Tabby would come back to me, as a bigger dog and a protector, and I felt some relief. I bathed her and I, together, and anointed us with lavender oil, to ready us each for the departure. I cleaned and saged the house and the blankets we would use when the veterinarian arrived at our home for the passing. Ryan slept on the couch each night and I pushed our bed up against the wall and lined the floor around us with pillows in case she fell off without me waking in the night. I sang her to sleep, and with her softly snoring beside me, I wrote poetry about gathering my strength and courage for the morning of.

I held her tight in my arms through the whole thing, and it was both the most beautiful and shattering experience I've ever had. When the doctor carried Tabby's still body away that morning, I sat frozen by the window and watched him gently lay her in the backseat, wrapped tightly up in the blanket I had sent her away with. The blanket was one my mom had given me several years before. When the car turned the corner and I could no longer see them, I turned to Ryan, and I looked at him and he looked at me and in that split second, I felt a choice and I knew it was a gift Tabby had just given me. I chose to collapse into Ryan's arms and release what was inside. I wailed and I shook, and he held me with all his might and then something transformative happened. He wailed and shook with me. And in that moment, I knew I wasn't alone; I knew I no longer had to choose to be alone.

I walked through a passage that day, with Tabby, and since, I've been feeling my way through this new space. I've been releasing to the flow of the river current and saying goodbye to all the parts of myself–all the moments in time–that Tabby saved me from, that she witnessed and participating in my surviving.

This collection of poetry contains captured moments of this pivotal release. The lines on the pages hold clues and keys into this process of surrendering to suffering; of letting it overtake you and die off the parts of you that you don't need to hold onto anymore. It's both beautiful and gut wrenchingly painful. But it's life. And I wouldn't have it any other way.

PART I

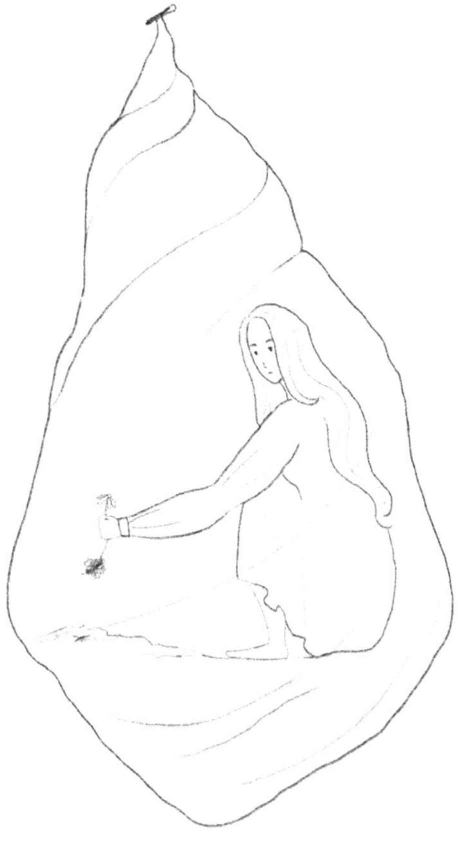

PURGING PAIN

The first part of this book mirrors my own journey of acknowledging and releasing pain in the first few months following Tabby's passing. Through my own process of mourning her and coping with the grief of her loss, I found myself facing memories of trauma and abuse from my past. It was as if her death triggered something inside of me; it summoned me to make a choice to embrace my own metaphorical death. Because she represented solace and peace for me, letting her go meant letting go of the shield she was and digging up all the things I had buried under her comfort. My metaphorical death meant I had to face painful parts of myself I had kept hidden and buried for many years.

Following her death, I found myself facing difficult emotions like rage, hatred, regret, and sadness. But it cut so much deeper than just losing a cherished pet. From deep within my psyche arose memories of trauma from my childhood, from my time in the military, and new understandings of how those traumas impacted my life in the present. The poems in this section reflect this dance with pain I navigated during the initial shock of no longer having Tabby physically in my life.

The poems represent my internal process of purging pain I had held onto for too long.

They address mental health conditions, addiction, and shadow selves. But because healing is not linear, this section also includes poems that embody joy, humility, and self-growth. Amidst the ground-shattering pain that was surfacing for me during this time, the elusive joy I felt was that much sweeter when I did feel it.

Please note, there may be poems within this section (and throughout the entire collection) that are triggering for those who contend with mental health issues, trauma, and/or addiction. Some poems express emotions related to depression, anxiety, Post-Traumatic Stress Disorder (PTSD), eating disorders, sexual and emotional violence, and addiction. Please take care of yourself as your work your way through this poetry collection. And most importantly, know that you are not alone. None of us are ever alone.

August 3, 2021

Raw

I feel so raw and vulnerable,
just open
for the world
to see,
pierce,
take me,
hurt me,
abuse me,
set me on fire.

Consume me,
but then
leave me alone.
Leave me quietly
sobbing
on my own
to heal.

To find all the pieces
scattered about.

With my glue
the sticky of life
I will put it back
together again.

Me back;
re-turn
to a new

self
made even more
beautifully
than before.

August 4, 2021

Free

You go up
always cum
back down.

But UP
first
for a while,
a long while
I'll stay.

Riding,
surfing,
surfacing,
oh shit,
so much
much, much, much,
make it stop
too much too quick
no rest;
moderate.

A voice
yeah, I hear you,
appears
and tells me
my truths.

You take away my pain.

Hold me inside,
keep me inside,
cancel plans,
stay home,
don't go,
stay with me
consume me.

Blow it out, cough
harder
more, more, more.

I'll miss you
old friend
but you
can't have me
anymore.

I'm free.

August 11, 2021

Red

I hurt and
blood red
anger seeps
from my veins.

It didn't start with you
and it won't end with you.

But you
make it worse
with your silent complicit-ness.

Fuck you,__________, for not
seeing me.

Fuck you,__________, for not
hearing me.

Fuck you, Uncle Sam, for not
protecting me

like you wanted
me to do
for you.

August 17, 2021

NAME

I named it.

I didn't even know
it was there
to name.

I mean,
I knew
when the panic attack was rising
up my stomach
into my chest
restricting my throat
from breathing.

I knew
when rising
from the couch
to shower
was my big win
for the day.

I knew
when I hit it again,
and again,
and again,
hoping to smoke myself
into a realm
of unknowing innocence.

I knew
when I ate and ate and ate
until it came back up
spewing
into my sink.

I knew
when I didn't care
what his name was
only that he
would ravage me up
harder, faster, dirtier
until the same
darkness
filled my soul from the pussy up.

I knew
when I couldn't connect
couldn't feel
couldn't see
or be seen.

I knew
when they
were sharing
their stories
and it was
my story too
and I could no longer

hold it in
stop myself

from leaking
from looking
into the mirror
staring me into the soul.

My soul touched, tainted,
fractured
by Him.
A broken Him.
All of them Him.

August 24, 2021

Rage

The rage
is eating me
swallowing me
I can't see
straight
any longer.

I scream
my lungs will tear
as the dark
pit of despair
claws its way
through my being.

I cannot tolerate
any more of
this treatment
this existence
this life
of half living
of barely being
of inadequate existing.

I loathe
the meaninglessness
the purposelessness
the coasters.

I fury

my brow
at the belittled
disempowered
souls.

Why be here?
Why do I care so much?

Why can't you
do better?

Why can't we
do better?

I hate
in my heart
an unexamined life.

Intolerable pain
comes from the
lack
of self-truth.

I am done.
No more.

September 15, 2021

Listening

My body is demanding
I rest
sink into the solitude
and take head
of all my possibilities.

Releasing urgency
surrendering to stillness
opening to opportunity,
I wait
to receive.

A messenger,
a do-er,
a see-er,
what calling
did I choose?

Inner knowing
ensures
the fruits
sewn
of my labor.

Yet,
the choice
is mine
and mine
alone.

For God
lives
in me,
through me,
as me.

God creates
my path
from
the gumption
of ecstasy.

And it is there
which I fuse
all that is,
all that will be,
all that was.

Time knows
no bounds
in the inner realms
of whole
Truth.

Yet here
in the now
it is only I
with my choice
to know myself

and God
with creation

of truth.

Shhhh,
I'm trying
to listen.

September 21, 2021

Dis

I am
a disabled Veteran.

Am I
dis-abled?

What's that mean?

Feels mean,
like a dis.

Does it
make life
harder
to go
and get up
and forge ahead
brilliantly?

Or do memories
of a time, place, thing
that happened
share the gift
of choice
to arise
for dis-pair?

September 26, 2021

Sun Day

The beauty
of Sun day
softens me.

I am awake
as the Sun warms
this
now
here.

The fire
inside me
beckons
to the rays
caressing my cheeks.

Kitty meows
car drives by
wind dances
with the tree limbs
and all is well.

All is here
lively, awakened.
Thank you,
solar complexity,
for this gift.

September 29, 2021

Friendly Foe

I feel it again
familiar old friend.

Maybe foe
it's hard to know.

Yes or no,
maybe so.

She feels god-like,
strong

punching me
from within

a space
vaster than I.

I wish not
for lies
burn me.

It's loud,
chaotic
clarity sees.

Gibberish
full of null
truth.

What's under here?

She is
He is
they are.

I miss them
so fucking much

I can hardly
let it in

or I might just
implode

into sad nothingness,
alone.

So, I go on,
next, please.

I feel more IN me
to stay far without.

One for the other.

I can't be
with you

because
of how much

that stings
me, too.

Can't help
can't fix
can't save

from the assured
inherited sins

suffering
I still can't name

but I notice
it there

finding its way
to me.

October 2, 2021

Cracks

A label
elicits
things defined
by the docs
that dictate
a meaning
of me.

Of my moods
my nerves
my actions
inactions
and participation
with life.

Name them
name it
first
so shall I heal.

But naming it
means it's real
it happened
it *is* happening
it's there
and once it has a name
can I not see it
anymore?

Can I choose
to ignore?

Suffer in silence
evade and avoid
save myself.

God won't let me
do that.

Love asks me,
invites me,
to surrender
to the cracks
inside of me
leaking
with all the
stuff
of living.

All the choices
I did not make
but rather,
I survived.

Crack it open
life says,
and move and shake
so it pours out
of me
and cleanses me
anew.

Name it
so I can
damn it
away
away
away
be gone
and let be.

This power,
learning,
growth,
healing,
it belongs
to ME.

So name it I shall,
I must.
I will
into existence
a future of free
a moment
of Me.

October 6, 2021

Take

I dream
of you
of the dark
disgust
deep in your soul.

It moves me
every single time
the energy emerges
and once more
I remember.

It all
overtakes my body
frozen with fear,
suffocating in shame,
paralyzed

by the pit
in you
that digs into
the innocence
of me.

From every dream
I wake
to a knowing
of an unspeakable
truth.

And I
am angry.
I am loathing.
I am sorry
for you.

What it must be like
to exist
in your sleeping state,
your harming hate
of you.

I try
to forgive
but
it's complicated,
you see.

With each wake
I remember
again and again
what you took,
what I have

yet to heal
and every time
I hate you
a little more
you take.

My dream
at stake.

My life
on hold
while I manage this,

tend to that,
oh wait, more to heal
because you steal
what was never yours
to have, to feel.

Sometimes
I find
some light
I always
wake

but never full,
never whole
for a forced delight
shall cum
once more.

October 10, 2021

Truth of Me

What is my truth
and where,
dear love,
do you hide?

From me,
taunting me
with your
whispers

of what was
and imprinting
that which
will be.

I can't see you
and feeling is diluted
with all the stuff
that was.

I know
no way
out.
Only here

in this unknowing
shall I dig my heels
into
this shallow

Earth.
The dirt
so moist and fertile.
And find my way

back home to myself,
to the answers
of the questions
I quiver to ask.

But I must,
or I'll never
know, feel, see
me.

October 15, 2021

NOW

I've been searching
for truth
and it's been hard
to find.

Too much
wide open space
yet never enough,
too.

Both feel confused
by what I know or
think, or do,
maybe be.

I keep to hear
inside is where
I'll find
that damned truth.

But it's easier
always
each time
not to look.

Do
something else
evade, ignore
ya know, all that.

More and more
I'll find.
But no truth,
none here

to see.
Only whiskers,
rain,
and herstory.

My story.
This one
that I'm writing
right now.

October 16, 2021

Fun Guy

Playing, popping up,
prancing & plugging.
You, my friend,
my lover,
and us,
well, yes.

Yes, please.
I'll have some more
get me up off
this floor
to grow,
to connect,

to talk between
the trees
and lie naked
in the backyard Earth
where you cover me
with flowers.

We giggle
and tickle
a sweetness
so light and young
bringing up back 'round
one by one.

October 16, 2021

Sounds of Saturday

Teddy's lullaby,
lover's soft snores;
we click our tongues
and call for kitty.

Coffee pot gurgles,
my pen strokes,
light sneaks through
the fall frosted window

and all is well.
Well is abundant.
This present
is mine.

October 18, 2021

HOW

How
do I heal
from this
quote on quote
    "trauma"?

How
do I heal
from something
so dirty
inside of me?

From Him
looking at me
looking into me
with a disgusting lust
that crawls on my skin?

From Him
not seeing me
not seeing Her
never, ever even
being willing to look.

How
do I heal
from pain
so deep and far inside
no one knows it's there?

He violated.
He vomited
his own tar
into
my open sky.

How?
How can I forgive?
How can I heal
something so sinister
something so real.

There is no happy ending here.
There's only me
warming in the sun
my pen wildly dancing
letting it out.

October 18, 2021

Cadence

In unison,
I belong.
Marching,
left always first.
Not me, not you,
just our left,
together,
the same.

Didn't matter
our why.
Only that
we said *yes*
and we signed,
and so there
we were,
in unison.

You saw things,
I know you did.
I feel it
in how
you be
with me,
with everyone,
with yourself.

When you see
things

they low crawl
into you.
It's hard to see them not.
Just look left
and maybe then
you can, see.

If it's not
too late
all ready.
Whatever it was,
I saw
it too
if even
only in you.

Not you,
not me,
remember
it's a 'we,'
so left foot forward
and there
we
will be.

October 18, 2021

Silly Sun

The sun is dancing
a mirage of colors
for me.

And the sky blue
is so vast today
it's like pure silk

caressing through
every break
in my skin,

filling me
into a hazy daze
of bliss serenity.

This feels
warm and light,
playful

as the leaves twirl
in the spectrum
of rays.

My toes
are wiggling
through the wind.

Bzzzz,

a bee comes
to smile with me.

And there's the train
whistling
to let me know

my love
is cumming
home

back
to me
once and again more.

How wonderful.

October 20, 2021

FALL

Fall is for forward
motion in play.
It's for the messages
from what was
to what
will be.

Fall is strong
and she has blue hair
carries a torch of fire
sparkling the places
the sun is not shining
anymore.

Fall brings forth
the dark
that we all
seem to fear
yet she has a secret
quiet beckons to hear.

It's change
far and near
it never stops
not even
for you,
my dear.

So let fall be,

she's here to do a job.
It's to still your go,
surrender to flow,
accept what you know,
open to show

the spaces
between
you and me
and all
of what
shall be.

October 20, 2021

Transfix Me

Shine on me
and show
what's inside
this forming dream
I make.

Glow golden
and charge us
with a jolt
of the luminant.

Humble us
as we lay before you
with this open flame
he built for me,
for you.

Transfix
and open me
unto you,
and him,
and us.

Take a silver sliver
of my heart
so I can
have it back again
graced with your face.

So many faces you make.

Hold steady,
I feel you teach,
ride the tides
I pull
inside of you.

Lace up
the moment
and wait no more.
Live now,
together.

October 20, 2021

Luna-Tick

Seduce me, moon.
Let your glow
drip
between my legs.

Your shine
caresses the hairs
standing erect
on my skin.

Grab me with force
to awaken
the fire you charge
with your rays.

Aroused,
I throw my head back
absorbing the heat
from the sky
you own.

Luna-tick, tick, take
and make
me up
for this play.

Please, I beg
for more of this opening
summoned through the light

you pour from the heavens.

Save me
with a bow
of ecstasy.

October 20, 2021

Kissing Moon

The fire in the moon
holds us here
in this moment
between time.

Unknown of what's next,
unsure of forward,
confused of consciousness.
It's all too much,

often.
Until now,
here
with the floating,

flying embers
and the running clouds
playing peak-a-boo
around Luna.

We look
at each other
deep with eyes,
deeper with hearts.

It doesn't matter
none of it does.
Quite simple,
really.

To choose
to kiss
and enjoy.
That's it.

October 22, 2021

THROUGH

I am dying.

I have been
since you left
me here
alone
trying to cling
on to what happened.

I tremble
through gasps of breathing,
missing you
in missing the sanctuary
I hid in
in you;

that door
we walked through.
I can't find
anything
in this new
room.

I'm purging so much
through this portal
we opened
together
when you left,
when I left.

You anchored me.
Now, where is
my anchor?

I'm fleeting.
It's all moving so quickly.
Water running
it all down
my cheeks
out of my soul.

Help.
Please ask
God
to catch
me.

October 22, 2021

HATE

Fuck you.

I hate you.

You killed me
    as my childhood
was robbed
with your fists
pounding on my door

your rage
    seeped into
my veins
and pulsate
through my own limbs now.

I fucking hate you
        for the lack
for your inability,
unwillingness,
incapacity

to love me
and protect me
    from your own
        demons
consuming your soul.

You're a fucking monster
abusing the weak
  so you can feel a tiny fraction
of power
and control

in your pathetic
existence,
your sorry
excuse
  of a chosen life.

You do not deserve
you do not get
  my love
    my affection
  my trust

because you fucking stole it
already
when you tormented
my growing fragility
of my youth.

I fucking hate you
so much
that I can't feel it at all.

So much that my own
body, mind, and soul
did your job for you
and make me forget
your harm.

All of this hate
burns.

And in the ashes
is an unbearable
truth.

That I don't hate you
because of how much
I fucking love you.

Because of how much
I have always
only
simply
easily
just needed you
to love me,
too.

October 22, 2021

MESS

I think
tomorrow
I'll clean up.

Wash the dishes,
fold these blankets,
put the things away.

I'll do my chores,
lift and pour, shine the floor
once more.

I think
tomorrow
I'll get up,

wipe up
the sticky I spilt
with my wobbling hand

the day before.
I'll open
the curtains,

turn on a song
and move around
just a bit.

I'll vacuum
the rug,
clean the mirrors,

maybe
I'll sage too and
purify

this air
keeping me
living.

I won't do it now.
No,
for now

it's all just fine,
it's all ok
this mess of mine.

I'll let it be
sit here,
still

and help
my body
release.

Part II

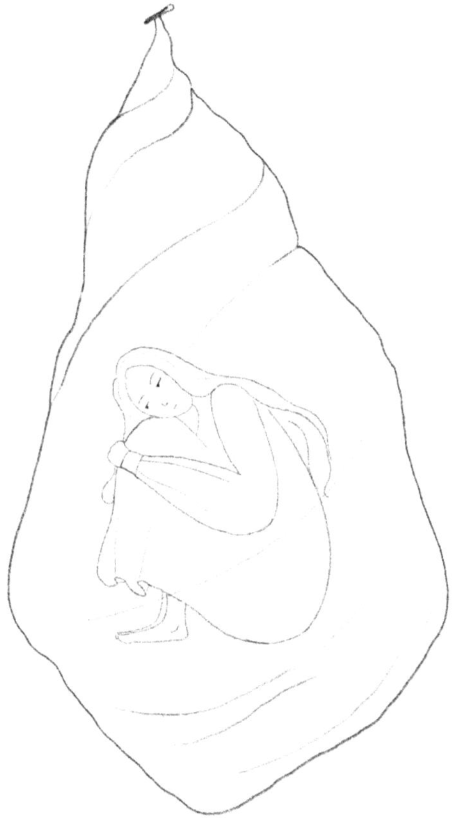

Giving Grace

After my initial few months of giving voice to the deep pain within, I entered into a space of grace. I recognized I was changing and healing and so I leaned into the stillness, quiet and solitude I was craving at the time. I cocooned for this next part of my journey with death.

The poems in this section represent a state of limbo. I was neither here nor there but found myself between (metaphorical) dying and rebirth. I was not ready to fly yet, but I knew I was doing the necessary work of preparation. I used poetry to cope through recovery of addiction and mental health battles. I understood joy was around the corner, but that I wasn't quite there yet. I felt a disparity within–I did not yet know union between my mind, body, and soul. And so, I focused on the difficult work of giving myself grace and trusting both in myself and in the process I was surrendering to. The poems in this section reflect this process of learning to trust myself and lean in and once again, illustrate that healing is a cyclical journey.

October 26, 2021

COFFEE

Sunshine is rising
up
over the neighbor's roof

and I'm feeling
so cozy
in this holding chair,

this blanket
squeezing me
while I sip.

There's not a sound
to here;
total silence

fills up the air
just humming
from the morning light.

October 28, 2021

Don't Know

I don't know
what to do
anymore.

I ache
for the familiar
my body

is screaming
and kicking
to let go of.

There is
no going
back.

I know
this truth
so well.

My knees
want to sit by you
on the couch

and touch
your skin
how we used to.

But I can't
because
those days,

those
good old days
they've passed.

Right now,
your knees
aren't here.

Only mine
touching
my confusion

about what's next and
I don't frickin
know anything.

Except
that I
don't know.

November 1, 2021

ALL

I don't
just die.

No,
there's more
than that
alone

for dying
reveals
a door
unknown

to many
but the soul.

The soul's been there
time and again
no big deal,
says she.

We'll go for a bit
then we'll return
really simple,
you'll see.

Fear not
to release,
open up

and feel,

feel all you can
you know
nothing
is real.

It's all one big stage;
all the poets,
sages
and wise ones

knew
we make up the rules,
we get
to choose.

Select the twists
and the turns,
our pain and sorrow,
too,

the moments
filled with ecstasy,
all our bliss
beginnings.

Choose it all,
skip over none
this isn't all just
about having little fun.

Life is it

all;
death fills
this truth.

November 2, 2021

Stilling Skies

Calming quiet
overtakes
me and this
and now.

Captured
by
this serene
stillness.

Hush,
there's nothing
here
to see

only being
wrapped up
in this
warm moment.

This soft blanket
swooning me
to succumb
to a lull.

It's not dull,
no.
It's wise
to freeze

and
commune
with the crystalline
skies.

Words
can't always
be
found.

So close
your eyes
and
feel it.

November 2, 2021

Trapped

I feel
trapped
behind
this invisible wall.

Trapped
by the aching
and longing
for more

for always
one more
day, one
more time.

By the fog
rising
and covering
my sense.

Trapping
my self
exactly where
I am

not wanting
to move
not wanting to
find forward

because
why
should I
when back is

always
around,
always having
my back.

I am trapped
from those moments,
exchanges
inter-actions

of me,
trapped
in a scene
I can't erase.

That's what it is.
That's addiction,
that perpetual
trapping

from then
to now
to tomorrow.
Traps set

to catch me
again
forever
under it.

November 2, 2021

Up

It does
take you high
up and over
the parts within
that feel like
pins sticking.

There's not
a ladder
of words
and lists
and curses
in my mind.

It's all just
air
fluffy clouds
lifting me
up
over it all

so I don't
have to
fall
over
all
this mess.

I am

afraid
of heights,
my body says
'no, thanks.'

I'll stay down
where
I'm safe.

So then
what to do
with these
strong hands
pushing through
my eye?

Breath.
Just breathe,
and touch
the floor.

November 2, 2021

Go

I can feel
mind-body-soul
all three
not
together
but instead

ripped away
from that
ancient, omnipresent
peace
of
yog.

My body
doesn't know
how to
say no.

My mind
is angry, ashamed,
she's sad,
can't think straight
enough
for forward.

Spirit though,
she knows the way,
she always does,

but she can't
absolve free
will.

Circles
keep spinning
around
so, I suppose
I'll just grab
on
and
go,
one of
these times.

If I
just
hold on
long enough,
I'll meet
and
mend.

November 3, 2021

Okay

I'm in a cocoon.
I made it myself.
It feels safe,
cozy, warm, hugging me
carefully, slowly,
without avail.

It's here for me
providing peace
always and entirely.
It keeps
others away
when I don't want

to play
or go out
or be about
anything
other than
this solitude.

Guilt knocks
at the door
often
when I'm in here
but I don't answer.
No.

Rather,

I shut
the blinds
instead
and stay
in

here
alone
just a little
while
longer.
Is that ok?

November 3, 2021

Fly

There's something
inside of me
that I feel
living
off of shadows
from the forest.

I didn't put it there.
Everyone else did,
I think,
but maybe,
probably,

I said
yes
though
wanted
to say
no.

It's a web,
makes itself
a new string,
shoots out
from under
one already there,

all weaving
tightly

into a giant
chaotic
knot
that ties me

up
and down
keeping me stuck
like a fly
scared of
the spider.

Precipice,
and I again
choose not.
It takes
so much
to fly.

November 3, 2021

Funk

I've been
in a funk
and it's strange
down in here.

I know it
well
deep down
the dark hole.

I've peered
into it,
sat,
leaned over it

too many times
before.
I've bore
the weight

of it,
reluctantly.
I got it
from Her.

November 3, 2021

NEW STATE

I'm not
quitting
or
going without.

I am,
however,
choosing something new
and different.

It's simply a state
of consciousness
overtaking
the other.

November 4, 2021

Swoon

De-press-ion
is like
a pressing
down
in my soul

touching every
living part
of my being.
It's dull
nothingness,

sad un-maned,
unnamed
despair.
Quietly blank
with no sense,

no words,
no filling
in here.
My mind
tells me

it's only temporary
but I don't
believe.
No, I don't.

Because I've
seen it before
when I picked
Her up
off the floor

wiped the tears,
made the soup,
cleaned the house
and air
once more.

Nature or nurture?
Environment, genes,
trauma.
Who even fucking
knows?

Healing
eludes.
Sorrow swoons
me
today.

November 4, 2021

New Moon

Today is so quiet;
the sun
offends me
trying to shine
so bright
into me

when all I want
is to sink
into my sins
in the darkness.
I want to
fold over

the hushing,
lay into the void
and maybe
just touch
the edges
of this open space.

I'm tired.
The world is tiring
and truthfully,
I do not have
any giving
left
for today

or probably
not tomorrow
either.
I only want
to soak
in the chilling air

and feel
nothing
at all.

November 5, 2021

NEW DAY

This morn
I leapt to wake,
eager for the start
of this
new day.

It feels
the fog
has finally
lifted
and once more

I can feel
the cold
under my feet
as they touch
the floor.

A corner turned,
a door cracked,
a choice
made
for yes.

Part of me
left
and she's surely
been hard
to find,

all alone
up there
skimming above
the air
of our norm.

I grabbed on though
squeezed the railing
with all my might
and just
whispered

to my self
till it passed.
And here
I am
once more

finally
back down
from the top
of that
taking circle.

November 5, 2021

Bossing

I've chosen to make
this new road
where finally
I
get to be
boss.

Oh yes,
I get
to decide
the rules
of this game
now.

I set
the tasks.
I keep
the score.
I decide
which brick lays next.

I rise
early or late
yes, still
my choice
and then
I loiter

for a bit

soaking up
some morning dew,
sipping away
potions
for my day.

Just watching
the world wake.
I know
writing
is my way
to the top

of that rather larger
mountain.
Writing and
loving,
that too.
Opening up

get the lid
off
so spores
can take
flight
towards dreams.

Dreams I dare,
beginnings I bare
in this
bliss,
this life
I'm weaving

through
forcefully
with might.

November 5, 2021

HOLD ON

I could
not
get it
off
      of me.

It was like
this sticky
    numbing
    clenched onto
    my spirit.

My brain
was watching oddly
and scratching
his head
wondering,

oh my,
what
a sad,
sad
pickle.

My body was
like immobilized
with sad affect,
exhumed with
exhaustion.

There was
really
no choice
but to wade
and wait.

Latch on
to some hard,
hard and
sturdy
so you won't

fall
so hard
or lose
and get
lost abound.

If you
hold long enough
wave by wave
the fog eases
away gently.

November 6, 2021

LOSING & GO

For awhile
I lost my way
oh, I really got
        turned around.

I sat in a storm
crying about
walking in circles
by day.

I wove my hands
through the dirt
with a pen
scribbling

my minds
seed
and
dead.

I made
lists and I
wandered
a lot

not knowing
what
shall
I do.

Anguished with anger,
rupturing with rage,
exploding energy,
out it all went.

Scary and lonely
and homey
and cozy
it's been.

It hurt
real bad;
it still does
some

but I've
made
up
my mind.

Onward,
I go
from
here.

November 7, 2021

HIGH

I am
an addict.
And that's
hard
to say.

But I must.
I trust.
That when and with
the brute

force
of a name
my forward
will change

to a world
not this same.
When I am
not high

I'll soar
then
higher than
before.

I'll climb
to the top
over this

play

holding my
feet
down
into hell.

Yes, hell.
A misery
locked into
no single

way out
but up high
one way
or another.

Might as well
choose,
create,
claim my way.

Part III

Choosing Choice

The next section of my journey (and of this collection) is a turning point; it's when I realized that I am in control. After the difficult work of purging pain and giving myself grace, I came to realize that everything is about choice.

The poems in this section embody freedom, expansion, creativity, and healing. They showcase sovereignty and empowerment. I was breaking open my cocoon and learning to own my suffering and to integrate my shadows. I began filling with gratitude, embracing sisterhood, and cutting cords of that which no longer served me.

I began to befriend death. I came to understand that fully living was dependent on fully embracing and integrating dying. The two are one in the same.

The poems in this section reify this newfound truth and my choice to continue choosing my voice throughout the healing process.

November 7, 2021

This Mourning

This morning
I woke
to softening
sheets
holding me up,

the sun
moving around
my window
behind the
flowered sheers

above where
kitty lay.
You beside
    me
curled up

into, around
        me.
I feel you
from
last night

when *we* were
me.
I could see
the colors
    dazzling

in the rays
gloating
and holding
in my cycs.
Never a

bliss
so full,
a moment
so whole

as this.

Merry Me.

November 7, 2021

Me

I am afraid
to be
    Me
to live
    My
truth.

Because
what if
they laugh or
cry, or
tell me
to die,

hate,
not appreciate
envy, steal, take
what I
know
is real.

I am
aching
to expand,
to be high
as me
goes,

to fulfill

my
destiny.
I must only
re-member
who I am

to contain
the soothing
of looking
back
to the paths
I've crossed

and nodding
a little,
smirking,
because wow,
holy shit,
me oh my,

I've done it.
So much of it.
All, really.
Well, most.
I'm here.
I've lived and

learned
as they say
and my truth
be told, is that
heaven is
Me.

Only me.
For me.
As me.
Within me.
Of me.
Me.

November 10, 2021

Set Free

Addiction
is seeping
out of me,
waking me
in the night.
A knot
in my stomach
aching and churning.

This throbbing
behind my eyes.
Exhaustion
I just cannot
escape.
Fog when
I think
withdraw

is almost over.
Nope,
more to come
out
of me
as I set
myself
free.

November 13, 2021

Toxic

Torture me,
withdraw
all my sense
has got
to be
better
than this.

Anything
sets
me off
and I can
always justify
in my clever
mind.

But barely
I sense
my soul
pleading for me
to soften,
relax,
be

and let be
while this
toxic
finds
its way

out
of me.

November 13, 2021

Sorry, Love

I'm sorry
my love
for this
hatred
spilling from
my heart.

It's not meant
to be for you
or at you
and it's certainly
not because
of you.

You
are the only
man
my swelled
heart
can touch true,

open with undue.
So then when
the past
unravels
and I kilter over
in hurt,

I conditionally

expect
you to know
how to fix
heal,
save me.

But
how silly
and cruel
of a rule;
nonsensical
that is.

This isn't
your fault
and I'm sorry
and I'm
grateful
for you.

November 14, 2021

This Here

Take pleasure
in this simplicity.

No need
for up, down,

always turned
around

chasing a rush
of existing.

The quiet
hush

of this
here now

reminds me
of a time long ago

before I knew
enough pain

to crave
and wane

for an escape
of now.

November 14, 2021

Regrets

I don't
regret
what happened

to me,
because of me,
consequentially.

No,
I really
do not.

Why
would
I?

When in the end
it was the living
that did me in.

For all
the capacity
of knowing

truth
is between
those lines

of

wise
learnings.

November 14, 2021

ONE

Open
and see
what cums
out
as I re-member
me and
why and
what
I am
here for.

No more
of that
petty
shame
or guilt,
loathing
or sulking
or even
forgetting
any–more.

No,
says I
and God,
Goddess,
all
of Them.
That's not

what this
living
is for.

But wait
because
actually,
it is.
    Pain
    plus
    purification
    produces
    peace
say what?

You
heard
me.
The
    profane
and
the
    profound
are
one.

November 14, 2021

CREATION

Sex
u
al
it
y
climbs
up
the spine
of mine
emerging from
the whole
womb
or
seed,
whichever.

It's not just
for fucking.
No, too
simplicity.

Creation
not solely
of the
child.

Rather,
chills up
the spine,

again.

It's for
c r e a t i n g
the and
our

experience
of god and
all there is
and isn't.

Got it?
make it.

November 15, 2021

Dear Sisters

It's not our fault;
it's not your fault.

You weren't traumatized
harassed
assaulted
raped.

No, it's cause of
No
action nor inaction
you took.
No!

It was Him or Her or They
that did it.

You weren't traumatized.
He traumatized *you.*

When he crossed
the line
stepped,
stormed,
over it,
over you,
over us.

We needed

our Uncle Sam
whom we swore
to protect
with all our might,
our strength,
our selves.

But when
I signed,
when you did,
I never agreed

I never even
fucking knew
how dangerous,
how true

the causes of my,
of our
service
would bare.

I am sorry
for you and
for me and
for what it must be

to always hold
this truth
without capacity
to see.

I am sorry
no one told us

what to expect
of the prevalence,

the wreck
that arises
under the
green.

I want you
to know,
sisters,
to see

Me
and to let me
see you,
too,

so together
we
may just
cum undone,

unglued,
unhinged,
unfiltered
in our storms

of rising through
naming
yelling
claiming

UP.

November 16, 2021

QUEENS

I am among
   Queens
who tear open
the ugly
broken frays
of evil.

Women who
not just
rise up
but build, claw,
climb, lift
up

one by one,
story by story,
silence by speaking

to the rage,
fury,
shame, guilt, crumbles
held,
locked away in that pit
of our souls.

When we
open the lid
on this super-glued shut jar,
creation forces

pushes, dances, leaps,
tiptoes out

and there we are,
seen
being the queens of
our own
rights, lives, futures

and we see,
hand-in-hand
how to rise.

November 20, 2021

TWIRL

There's a feeling here
underneath
a lot of mess
and pain
and suffering that was.

I've been
so tired,
so long.

But now,
after creation has flown
from my loins,
there's a breath,
so fresh

of juvenile joy I'm sitting
with, unfolding into
an enchantment by.

Finally, I think I could play
kickball again

and twirl and spin
and just maybe,
everything'd be okay.

It will,
oh yes,
it will.

November 20, 2021

FIGHT

He's hugging me
and our kitty
is rubbing me
and now I can feel
the world
just holding still.

I'm filling with
glee,
happy as can be,
wishing
this moment
eternity.

The fire is warming
the sky clouds
are storming
and peace
is abound
in this now.

I'm comforted,
I'm safe
I am ordained
by grace;
what a serene blessing
for me.

Oh thank you,

all gods
for bringing me
here
to a love
overflowing with might.

I've learned,
I've grown,
I've wailed,
and I've shown
living is worth
this fight.

November 22, 2021

Sacred Season

Sacred, ancient
bleed,
what will we
re-lease
today?

What is
worth
a sacrifice
of undoing
for becoming?

Which lessons
are asking,
un-lining
to be
taken head?

Oh, bleed
bless me
as I open
and out pours
the pains

full of wisdom
and height.
Impart, please
into me
new seeds

for marrow
and the pending
turns to come.
Thank you,
Mother Flow

for this sacred
season.

November 22, 2021

Top

Finally,
I am here.
After so long
of a hunt,
an anticipated
arrival awakens
me each day,
summoning me

to play
and make
and exceed
any unjust
impositions
impoverishing
my Me.
I've found god.
Silly She

been here all along
arms
(and legs)
wide open
and meticulously
and majestically
pulling Me
forth

into power.

No turn has been
left unturned.
No eye left
dry.
No heart made
out
all whole.

No,
it's never that
lame
or dull.
Goddess is full
of show.

So, please do
sit back and
gawk,
just watch me
          cum out
on top.

November 27, 2021

NOISE

There's too much
noise here
too much
drudgery
from way back when,
too much
keeping me
from going within

knowing my own needs, desires
voicing of my own worth.
Too much
of othering,
butting in,
insisting
I choose a way
appeasing them.

No, I say
after too much
silence.
No, I won't
succumb.

There once already was
too many times before
I could articulate
a mode of me,
a safety to be

able to firmly stand
on my own
    truth.

No, is what I
give them now
empowered with how
much work
has inched me
closer and closer
to freedom
from all this noise.

November 28, 2021

Smudging Heal

My body
has so much
to say.

She's angry, floppy,
tired
and not okay.

She's been
unwantingly touched,
seen,

condemned by
undoing
deeds within.

She's been hard
to tame
or to know.

She gallops around,
threatens
to leave town

if I don't
get it straight
soon enough.

But fickling

is true
so, I loosen the screws

and tell her
I'll be back 'round
next moon.

She hates,
screams,
hisses and hides,

unabashed by
kisses
no more.

I've had enough,
her whispers are
thick

and smeared with
a bold
finger smudge.

I try to hear
But I can't unsee
that smear

or unfill, unfeel
the pain
of this heal.

November 29, 2021

Owned

It's so painful
to go;
there is a place
pouring into
and out of
me
as I creep and run
away from you.

Tick, tick
tock,
it's gonna set
me off
and then
hours to days to weeks
of reeling it in,
bringing me back

piece by piece
from hiding,
escaping,
no hope
forsaken
as I mend
what broke
long ago.

Undoing these chains
weighed down

with pain
do you see why
I must just
say *no*?

I can never
re-turn
once I've already
left;
I've already tasted
this rest.

I'm so sorry you're there
it's not
for lack of care,
it's for preserving
all the broken
of me.

Please understand,
please try to see
I love you, I do
but you
may not
own me.

November 29, 2021

ICE

It got cold
once you knew
what for me
I claimed as true

and you took
a sharp dagger
and stabbed
eagerly.

On the edge
of your seat,
tapping your feat,
willing your own

demise.
There is
no blue
in your skies.

And that's not
my fault;
it's not
what our god taught.

This is inherently
your own devise.
So, ice me out,
really, do what you must

for nothing
will change
as I transcend
from fire to dust.

I owe you nil;
I'll answer no call.
This is my life,
you will take none at all.

Be
on your way,
let us part,
there will be no

permanent
absence,
for you reside
in my heart.

I love you, Mom,
and I pray
to infinity
that your storms calm.

November 29, 2021

Secrets

Father,
your secrets
are kept
no longer.
Your stares
are seen
by all.

Your hands
reaching and
pinching, are bound
for cut.
Your privilege
unearned,
is rushing out.

How dare you
for even one
tiny blimp of
our lives
believe you
would escape
the rapture

awaiting
in the mirror.
Here I am, Father.
Holding it up;
I've cleaned it shiny

clear as fucking
crystals

shall you stare
your own black sins
into eyes of coal
and know
the transpired evil
shall face
Queens of Justice.

And that heavy
scale will flip over
leaving you outed
in the open chill
for all to see,
for all
to kill.

So, die
with my sword,
I'll lick off
the blood
and smile
at these pearly
white gates.

December 1, 2021

Flying Bird

Today, I am flying
up over the fluffing clouds
alongside the
ravens, crows,
and the red cardinals.

My two feet are dancing,
swaying around
on this clean floor
and laughter erupts
from my eyes.

The earth has spun
around and
rotated with me on it,
moving along so
frantically and intentionally.

Until I got
to right here
in this glorious
Up I made
with my fierce palms

and my open wide heart,
the blue in the back
of my cleared throat
curling open
for my voice

to rise and
sing
as
a flying bird
does.

December 7, 2021

Honoring Her

On this day
I carve out time
to remember,
pause,
let myself rewind.

I look back
and I see
the greatest truth
man must know-
change is abound, so quietly.

I couldn't have stopped it
no matter how hard I held,
how many times I wished
for more
with my heart swelled.

I tucked my nose
into your ear
I inhaled your smell and
your love and
wisdom to hear.

We played and
we danced and
we walked, climbed and wept.
Such a journey we shared,
such a special time kept.

And then came the day
I had but one choice,
to fall to my knees and
call out
my voice

to tell you how much
you've led my spirit grown
how much
you've taken
me home.

Thank you, my girl
for all that we shared, for
showing me
my way
amidst my despair.

I'm never alone,
I always feel you near
barking and
dancing,
roaming the air.

Today I will feel
all that shows up
in honor of you,
I will fill up
my cup.

I'll raise it high
to the wind

in the sky
and smile through my tears
as I feel us both fly.

I love you, Tabby.

December 8, 2021

Clicked

Some thing
inside me
has clicked
and now
wondrously,
I know my forward.

I am unafraid
of it all.
No more limbering
when I'm lost.
No more numbing
when the dark knocks.

Death scares me
no more,
for I've seen
Her pour
long sharp claws
into breaths amiss

and direct them
to the path
of the saving forest.
And now,
with this bravery behold,
fully living unfolds.

December 11, 2021

Show

The black ravens crow
and the sunflowers grow
showing a way
I can see
my unabashed glow.

A white butterfly's wings
a tune within
the scene
of my drama
here to tell.

The stories and triumphs
of those twists
and wide turns,
an unfolding of all
that we know.

The world is a stage
our lives foretold
from guided knowing
unwinding my roads,
upheaving the no's

the yes' of grandiose
just flowering
as I take a
grand bow
once more.

Part IV

Honoring Home

And finally, after several months of navigating treacherous pain and suffering, I began to come home to myself. At this point on my journey, I started to imagine and move into my highest path. I started really knowing myself, my own needs and wants and I surrendered and released anything standing in my way of reaching them.

I began aligning my internal and external worlds, largely using poetry as a way to do so. I felt immense gratitude for the growth I was experiencing–which came only from shedding what was no longer for me. I walked away from the things, people, and places in my life holding me back. As one on my poems in this section describes, *I was ripping up roots just to grow them again.*

In this section, the poems tell my truth of being in a place where I felt a sense of home again. I knew my way forward and I was feeling both confident and grateful to leave the familiarity of the old and dead behind me.

December 14, 2021

Turns

The air is glowing
bright
through the corners
of my sleepy eyes.

Gods are reaching through
this light
so right
just for a moment

my eyes
will close and
my chin will lift and
be greeted

by a warm soothe,
and inner pull,
a wise know
of my next.

There's a time for rest,
a moment's upset
and then always
that jolly joy finds rise.

A seamless transition
of nature's recognition
that impermanence rules
this turning world.

December 14, 2021

Nature's Beast

I'm friends with a beast
tamed with timed feasts,
a wild fur softened
by pet.

Words don't belong here
in this realm of seeing love.
Eyes lock and expressed faces
talk

and my soul knows why
you're here.
Wise like an owl,
you prance and you prowl

but it's really for me
why you've come.
I think I tame you,
we both know it's untrue,

for it's you
who's teaching my way,
showing me when to rest,
when it's time to play,

how to open
my heart
undoing that rigid pain
of yesterday.

Moments of stilled
fluttered will alert
my impenetrable will
to know nature's order of things.

December 15, 2021

CLOSE

Rest has found me
quietly laid down
by my tired feet.

I've held still and waited
while my crooked body
opens and receives this deep heal.

Alone I've been not
with soul's always near
dying rest is made of no fear.

Cycles always go round
again and again balancing scales
death and birth are plenty.

I surrender to this know
comforted by the hushed slow
and my eyes close again more.

December 19, 2021

YULE

What is heard to stay
and what's asking me
to take away
and recycle to Gaia?

Another turn of the
year, cycles of constant
change brining me to
the core of
surrenderance

beholden to none.
A wild ride it's been,
love blossoming
within.
Heart's widening
mind's archiving
body's realigning

as I graze barefooted
on this land I may never own,
but tend, gently
and ferociously

wielding my wand
and speaking
with fairies
beyond mulberry trees.

I’m here for a while,
overcame the woes of
morrow, soul’s carving for a
hallow of this undone

dropped at my feet.
A weightless dance I greet
under the moon
full of Yule.

December 19, 2021

Wise Belly

Show your belly
to the sun,
roll around in the rays,
absorb that silly, innocent fun.

Lift to the air your wiggling toes
and opened palms,
catch the violet
in your eyes.

This moment of full receiving,
well, nothing
could ever be
more wise.

December 20, 2021

Dreaming Wake

Sleep eludes me
as I dream in full wake
of a harvest
awaiting my seeds.

Of mulberry trees
wildflower groves
and fruit hanging
for a midsummer's bite.

Of simpler days
time fully away
from this half life
keeping me still.

Of magic in the forest
a new life before us
promises
begging to bloom.

My mind's so adrift
blowin' dandelion spores a wish
of the fertile land
calling us home.

So, cum now, my love
let's waste no more precious living
take my hand,
for the full moon has risen.

We’ve somewhere to go
we’ve learning to know
the choice is ours
to reap.

I’ll stand here steady
demonstrating my ready
assured of your rising
from sleep.

December 25, 2021

CURSE

Am I cursed
of missing them
and of hissing them
away?

I overflow with anger
and grief
on celebratory days
like today.

So far away, such danger
to be near.
I am devoid
of holiday cheer.

December 27, 2021

Rest Ready

The day came and it went
and I will say, I'm relieved
to gain respite from it all.

Wanting to withdraw
inward towards a rest
and holding filling me back up.

It takes so much to give and
to receive and to be away so
I can stay here, unto me.

And this life full of new ways,
traditions, doings of the day
celebrating a time supposedly divine.

But now I just feel tired, drained,
not full of glee, not prancing around
merrily.

I think perhaps I can relate to this
cherished date split to honor
the death of an old, time of a new

birthed holy and true, to do the work of light
unto me and unto you.
Carving a path for all.

So then, yes, I imagine this exhaustion

is right, balancing of energy
that flew through the night.

Time to blow out the candles,
put the gifts away, settle your spirit
and rest ready for a new day.

December 27, 2021

Choose

I feel your wall
you built it so tall
scared so little and hurt.

Away from the ones,
from the crippling love
that kept you gone so long.

It's made us safe to say no
to learn these rooted words
that fill up our sad heart whole.

But this time came to pass
for not one truth will last
except what is known in the bones.

Cut open down the middle
use those strong mighty words
to solve this binding riddle.

Gather your peace off the floor
accept suffering no more
the choice is all we get.

So, choose it now
and choose it loud
this life if yours to live.

•

December 28, 2021

Wild Rivers

The turning wheel moves
once more through
the blowing wind and howling air.

Show truth in my eyes
reflecting ways back
in that frozen winter pond.

Spring nests will build
with moss collected
from pecking peaks

and tight hugs
flow mightily among the children
sitting at the feet of wisdom.

Currents get stronger
escaping no truth under the moon
showing off for the pine forest.

So please just still on this mountain,
wait for the red bird to land.
Trust fully, devoid of happenstance.

You will come to know
where it is you belong
among the rising sun
and the wild river dance.

December 30, 2021

Quiver Dark

Dance upon me
and stomp
and beat
these quivering feet.

Remove your heavy veil
let it slide down
your bare shoulders
with ferocious wail

out into the black sky.
Will yourself
to die
so the golden serpent

may rise up
your breathing spine
weaving the line
of knowing.

Claw off your disguise
stand bare and wise
and let the dark
swallow you whole.

Only then
can you
know
truth.

December 30, 2021

Embracing Heal

I still want you
between my lips
dragging long and deep

with a bitter inhale
harsh exhume
poisonous fumes

you sneaky bastard
I feel you creeping
I feel where you once were.

Okay fine, I'll close my eyes,
sit here still,
inhale the desire

fix this quill,
accept this fate,
embrace the hate

and heal.

January 8, 2022

MIGHTY LIGHT

I'll freeze no more
catching your misdirected roar.

I won't let you blame.
I won't cower in shame.

I reject your red hate,
your accusations of ungrate.

I'll overcome this inherited fear.
I'll open my soul to hear

the cries of the ones went astray,
the woes of this sorrowful day.

I'll inhale breath deep with might.
I'll walk fully towards the light.

January 12, 2022

HEALING SICK

I feel sick
as this disgusting pain
bubbles from the times
power was stolen in vain.

My tears are held back
because strong I must be
as I guide this healing
from the trauma of our military.

Step by step, story by story
opening hearts, souls, arms
reaching for more
overcoming such harm.

January 12, 2022

Everything

Incapacity to know
has taken hold,
interrupting my flow.

Have to do when I want to be
still, quiet, inward
away from the squeeze of this
productivity.

I feel a pressing
in my bleeding womb
shedding what was into tomb.

I want to close my eyes
just lay here for a while
release expectation to smile

ignore the hustle,
look away from the bustle,
just pull this warm blanket up over
my head.

Be here now
stop worrying about how
and trust everything's gonna be
okay.

January 14, 2021

Loud Stones

I'm releasing today
throwing stones out into the wind and
sprinkling my blood on the grave.

The one that held me in
held me back,
kept me down when

all I wanted was up,
to make our world just, better,
to ease the pain of my sisters and brothers.

I yearned to tell a truth
from grace, empathy, and generative
love.
I needed your trust. I needed your hugs.

But instead, another story wrote,
another way it went
that pushed me to my quit.

So, walk away I did
I left that place proud
and now I am here sharing

and my right
is to be
loud.

January 17, 2022

Rising Mother

Mama, where oh where
do you be,

rising up
from inside of me?

Homeplace, roots, ancestral lines
new and old stories
flying patterns with birds in the sky.

Down that old country road
we want taking us home,
parting us from the scare of unknown.

We're bound to high truth,
we've imagined it now,
looking and hunting as cats on the
prowl.

Gaia and Luna,
please show me the way,
take me to peace, help me to stay

unto myself in the midst of this dig,
ripping up roots
just to grow them again.

Releasing the old,
making way for the new,

oh, help me to see the past most true.

Help me to be bold,
loud and free
as I build this life for me

in the heartland, the homeland
the Earth
ripe with seed.

Help me to know,
help me to choose,
help me to commune and dance with the lose.

Help me to fly
with those wild birds in the sky,
help me to open,

to once again die.
To make way for this rise
of mother.

January 18, 2022

Moon Musings

Edgy wakings
Luna brings forth
this night
as I toss and turn.

Light
filled the dark
crevices
of the bedroom.

Up and out
I finally go
with a jar of blood
in tow.

My neck cranks
and I see her loudly
illuminating
the stillness abound.

Quiet surrendering
on this old,
odd moon.
Hush to hear no sound.

Made no big deal
but simple change
becoming real.
Pour out of that jar

yesterdays.

Times be gone,
holding begun,
just let me shift shapes
once again

from maiden
to mother hen.
Aching of potions,
dreams put to motion,

creation leaks
from my veins.
Pain transformed,
lessons transmuted,

glory made
with these palms.
Raise up my arms,
turn round my hips,

shake and swing
by new songs.
Oh moon,
keep playing your tune

and lighting up the eve sky
so bright with
love and peace,
stillness underneath

bygones

left in the night.
Swallow me whole;
I've somewhere to go,

pleasure to seep from these loins.
Spin one more time,
round back you'll be,
glowing this life of mine.

February 1, 2022

Accept Love

Hush now,
scared one
and hold steady
amidst the change.

Press your feet
down
into Earth
and ground
into the all-knowing.

You are not alone.
Nothing is forever.
Except Love.

February 1, 2022

You are Not

Going on a venture
into marrow's land,
got a lover by my side and
a kitty cat at my feet.

Purr, purr, purr
what have you done with Her?
Wisdom and fortitude
left no thing allude.

For alone you are not,
fear long forgot,
toes and spirit bare,
a magnitude of care.

You are a chosen one
in motion to becum
a warrior in all Her might,
a goddess diminishing fright.

February 2, 2022

Jump

You didn't jump in with me
that day;
too afraid
of the others at bay.

Locked in fear,
I can't get too near
or I lose myself too,
I become scared like you.

I'm angry, sad, numb,
not sure which direction
to go.

I'm freezing here with the snow,
wanting to let go
of the noise skewing my truth.

I hear the train whistle blow
as I heard before,
awaiting the return of my love.

Part V

Setting Space

I conclude this poetry collection sitting firmly in my own radiance and turn-on. This final section fully embraces untamed living and reifies alignment of my mind, body, and soul. The poems throughout this section represent a sense of arrival, of being found.

They speak of creating and sitting upon my own throne, of being far from alone, and of honoring my journey to and through this evolution. Yet, as seen throughout, life is not static, and healing is certainly not linear. This section also includes poems that express my trepidation and fear of fully stepping into this next chapter of new beginnings.

Within this new territory is peace and power, but it is achievable only through embracing both the might and the fright necessary to get here: death.

February 2, 2022

Mine

Drip sexy drop,
hips thrust on top.

Belly shakes,
legs embrace

breath quickens,
pleasure ripens

all across
these lines.

For this turn on,
it's mine.

February 8, 2022

Living

Full of missing,
heavy eyes
streaming
guilts of dismissing,
moments of reminiscing,
does it every get any easier?

Decisions of division.
Justification,
I need no permission.
Only from inside
where all this layering resides
do I need to be seen.

Only in my haunting dreams
shove my face in a pillow
bellow that scream,
release into the wild
that living
which shall know no tame.

February 9, 2022

It Is

I feel something new,
fully alive and true;
my mind, body, and soul
are dancing,
aligned in full.

Been a long time cummin',
spent many a nights numbin',
evading, escaping,
alone,
just tumblin'.

Then one day it all changed.
Life as I knew it
would never be the same.
A choice fell at my feet
and summoned me to greet

a forward of my own devise,
a reflection with no lies,
a knowing of my third eye,
a life away from hated high,
a creation made fully by *I*.

And so it is.

February 12, 2022

ARRIVAL

Hush goes thirty-two
widely opening for something new.
Appreciated lessons of old,
eyes and ears to the Earth
receiving the love of hold.

All my life has been
in preparation for this time when
I blossom and I bloom,
I become one with my moon,
on my way to ecstatic bliss.

Every crevice,
each miss
taught me what I need.
This is my year
I'm set to succeed.

Thirty-three welcomes me
with a white sky,
a warm tub,
my lover's arm,
this seeded farm.

I am here.
I've arrived.

February 12, 2022

Coloring Right

I'm gonna color
while I wait for you;
turn the sky pink
and Earth orange.

I'll pain trees purple
with black flowers
blooming berries
blood red.

I'll make birds white
and the rain green,
dried brown flowers
hanging from the walls.

I'll wait for you
as I color
this world.

Color it so bright
so alive
so right.

February 12, 2022

Us

Nothing ever so perfect
as now.

No concept–
no iteration
of a coherent how.

There shouldn't be.
Because really, *is there ever*?

It's just now,
just here,

just you and me.

February 14, 2022

After

Calm exudes,
love fumes,
adventure tunes
so serene.

Stress dissipates
meeting mates,
holding fates
freely full.

Wisdom transmutes,
coupling flutes
memories to boot
healing home.

Fluttering lingers,
interlaced fingers
overcome ringers,
arrival awaits.

I love you.

February 15, 2022

Found

Change is here,
storms rolling near.
Time to face the fear
of insidious unknown.

I can see my throne;
no longer am I alone,
afraid or begotten,
leaking of rotten.

No, I have faced the day.
I've found my way,
agreed to pay
the price of change.

February 16, 2022

Thanking Home

Thank you, my home
for what you've given me.
The shelter, the solace
the space to be free.

If walls could talk,
I wonder what you'd say
nodding at me,
a wink of fray.

You'd show me a scroll,
you'd let me see
the swaying of my life's unfold
and how it happened so gloriously.

Who I've becum under this roof,
the parts I'll leave here
decomposing and transmuting,
unraveling the past loose.

Thank you, brick road
for carrying my feet,
for carving my path,
for curating my heart.

I am home now.

February 17, 2022

Best Friend

I feel your soul
vibrating
on my lap

your soft fur
nurturing
my touch

your curious leads
peaking
my playfulness

your seeing eyes
telling
my way back home.

I feel your purpose
being here
is me.

February 18, 2022

Waiting Ice

Ice in the sky
twinkles bursts of light
in our eyes.

A dance of majesty,
a breeze of becumming,
we get to see.

It's sharp, and jagged,
cross under if you dare,
be limitless air.

Shine as this cold ice,
melt out in the open sky,
warmed by the blaring sun.

Sit still, too
and wait your
turn.

February 21, 2022

Scared Little

Catch me if you can.
Bet you can't.

I'm a little scared
for this whole thing.

Never gone this far,
never been this tall.

Letting go of control,
anticipation of old

being too hard to let go.
I am a little bit scared.

February 22, 2022

Magic Two's

Can you feel the magic today?
The alignment and magnitude
of pristine present-ness?

Of stars and planets dancing,
cardinals and ravens flying,
sunflowers growing?

Of new beginnings,
old ways re-membering.
Nothing amiss in this dream.

Can you feel the magic today?
The spark of a new day,
the bubbling up of play?

Of laughter erupting,
sensational touching,
a moment of being fully me.

Of walls crumbling,
waves tumbling,
newness seeping through the air.

Can you feel the magic today?
The ignition of hope in our hearts
found among creation of arts.

Of meeting again,

flamed twins
lighting candles for peace.

Of mountains moving,
snails snoozing,
nature alive and well.

Can you feel the magic
today?

February 22, 2022

GIFTS

Today calls us forth
becumming one,
becumming undone
by before.

No more shall we harbor
alone in somber,
filling our nets
with sand.

Stand
together and free,
there's space
next to me.

I invite you
to becum
what you've
always been.

Accept, embrace
this fated place
with all your might
and freight.

All of you
is welcome,
wanted
and well.

Drink from it,
nourish souls
folded and kept
between

seen
carefully undoing
those deeds,
not mine

but gifts of learning
I head,
I thank,
I am.

March 1, 2022

TRUE HOME

I am grateful for this floor
that's held me up right

for the walls
that dimmed the light

for this roof
sheltering me

for this garden
sprouting me anew

for the back porch
hearing my stories

for this bathtub
cleansing me whole.

I am grateful for this home
creating me true.

March 2, 2022

Becoming

Terror grips me,
holds me down
under the weight
of reaching
my dreams.

Cluttered chaos
fills the house,
fills my soul,
fills the spaces
between our love.

I don't know
what's next
after this day
or when I shall
again be okay.

Looming lesions
have taken hold
and now it's so hard
to get up,
to go.

Maybe you caused
or that did,
the thing
that isn't
me.

Old habits die hard
ya hear,
as new ways
inch by inch
come near.

So much turning,
my breath is cool
and shallow
as my own
fresh grave.

I'm mourning
who I was
and learning,
building
my becoming.

March 7, 2022

You Can Begin

Color between these jagged lines,
dance and sway to the tune,
of beginning again

on the road I painted red
this way, it points
to a sunflower tall at the end.

Betwixt is a rising
beckoning ceremonial rites
marked by the breath of Earth.

So, get the crystals,
pluck some flowers,
summon the moon's rays

and cry upon your alter.
Strip down to bare
the weight of beginning.

March 9, 2022

I Am Home

I made it
here
cozy and warm and full
of the living
that's always
been mine.

Of the making
intricately intertwined
in the frays
of the walls
and the creaks
of the worn floors.

Of the loving
so easy to cum
through the heart,
exploding with infinite
knowing
of a sacred secret

guarding these walls,
living in the wet soil,
holding the buried roots
of the pine in the back
growing sideways
up towards the sun.

Of the beautiful simplistic

peace abound
in the now
of this living,
of this loving,
of this home.

March 10, 2022

Unburdening

Why do you fear?
What do you hear
when peace, tranquility
come near?

My dear,
it's abundantly clear
the void, the vacuum,
they steer

you to tier
up
up
up

to take that big step
to peer over
the unknown.
Release your tears.

Veer into
the deep waters.
Rest your ears,
release ghosts of rear.

Come here,
unburden this fear.

March 12, 2022

I Surrender

I can feel the emotion there
lingering
on the other side
of this hazy succumb.

But I can't quite reach it,
can't let it in,
can't pour it through
my remembering body.

Of all the choices
I did not make,
the things
I did not say.

The healing
I did not feel,
the loving
I did not embrace.

Yet, here I am
just sitting still
in the smoke
bellowing.

Shame is serene
suffocation
summoning
surrenderance.

March 12, 2022

Living Life

Go now child,
make your alter,
lie upon it and
vibrate among it.

Pour your blood
onto this Earth
and sing to those
red and black birds.

Cross over,
your time is now
creation bursts
alive from your womb.

The sun and the moon
dance and
dangle
from your supple breasts.

Life this life
fully, euphorically
bathed in ecstasy
and ravenous tumult.

Come home
again and again
to your blooming, breathing and
be-withering self.

This,
dear child
is life
living.

March 14, 2022

Go

Finally let it go,
felt that flow,
saw my show,
heard to know.

Blew the gasket,
popped the top,
released
my pent-up steam.

Looked at my resist,
facilitated understanding
into ongoing persist.
I dismiss.

Instead, I'll be me.
I'll be free.
I'll intuit, channel, manifest
abundantly.

I'll remove this heavy,
sanctified and ready
to bow before my wild,
to voice my inner child.

March 24, 2022

Face

Tearing tears
to reface
about face
what happened.

My dreaming terrors
keep me
turning back.
No forward face.

Memories I'd rather not
until I must
muster up
to face.

Peace is proverbial,
fleeting and cruel.
Startle me
true.

Who am I
to claim victim
kept around
in unseen shadows?

Can hardly catch
my breath,
my rest,
my wholeness

with pasts of still,
still unnamed,
still flashing
to be tamed.

Anger fumes
like boiling acid
in my gut
bursting up.

Resolution knows no way.
Can't find a day
to march forward,
to put away.

March 30, 2022

The Pressing

The pressing is here
like a foggy haze, a dewy mist
that's steadily set
down heavily on me.

It comes slowly,
day by day,
hour by hour, even
until all I can do is exist.

All I can do is
survive and grip onto
the warm blankets I'm
hiding under, and hold on

for dear life, literally sometimes
as I feel the lifelessness
reaching up from inside of me
stealing all motivation to live.

My loved ones are kind
when it strikes,
patiently waiting and
gently nurturing me back.

An anger skims across the surface
of this lull, for why
must I carry this in tow?
Why must I endure?

Will I ever recover?
Will I ever truly heal?
Or will depression only falter,
only temporarily keel?

Exhaustion besets me today
and I make space around me
for self-compassion, self-kindness,
self-care.
Because I do care.

And I know this pressing
is a sickness, here to pass,
to slow and to show
some thing my mind's eye
cannot see in her busy-ness.

An inheritance of sorts,
met by a world outside
of my own devise
and together they aim
for my harrowing demise.

I'm tired. Have I said that?
It's worth saying again.
It helps me know when
I'm reaching a point, I'm lurking
too long over the void.

Alas, I'll close my book and put
down

my pen and muster all that I've got.
I'll bathe and wash clean
scrub this pressing off of me
and fan my flame of living.

And wait.
I'll wait for it to pass.

April 10, 2022

Cum and Dance

Sway and spin,
groove and bend

circle round
these hips.

Move those fingers,
tap, tap my feet

turn round my neck and
arch and groove my spine.

Dance and re-lease.
Find my soul

amongst this thumping
beat.

Shake it out,
toss round this hair,

wiggle about
no care.

Feel that tingle?
Catch it

and disperse.

April 10, 2022

Sunshine

Kiss my face,
freckle my cheeks
and warm me
from the outside in.

Pierce into my soul,
help me to feel whole,
and rescue me
from that cold winter's night.

Graze over my skin,
raise height to the chill
of the sweeping wind
and remind me of a time bright
again.

Let me bask in your glory,
steadily release my worry
and feel a reignition
of my flame lit once more.

Pamper my spirit,
oh sun, let me hear it
bright warmth
is lit at my door.

Stir up some magic,
brew potions of havoc
and let's just wiggle

our toes in this sun.

April 18, 2022

Believe

Recognition of this road.
Surely been here before,
surely carried this load.

Can I find a reason
if I search far and wide
how I got here again,
just tryin' to hide,

tryin' to feel better.
Release some stirred steam,
finding a way out,
running from my dreams.

Chronic is what my diagnoses read.
Depression, anxiety, PTSD, bulimia,
addiction to forever feed.
I am brought to my knees.

I am tired, angry, forced to leave
myself sometimes,
to survive,
to believe

pushing through supersedes.

April 22, 2022

Let This Be

Look around and see what's
before you.
Listen and hear the melody
of the chirp.
Quiet and open your soul
to your becoming dreams.

Let this be
the last night
of mourning

and deeply feel
the squeezing
as you squirm
out of your opening cocoon.

Know you've been where
you've been,
you've done what
you've done

only in service
to this become
into my bloom.

Let this be
the last night
of mourning

as I welcome the
cleansing moon
here to bleed
my past away

to be poured
into the soil,
over the garden
and woven into the Earth
with my two doing hands.

To plant new seeds
growing through
the cold darkness
towards the blaring light.

Let this be
the last night
of mourning

as I tune into,
vibrate alongside,
choose empathically
now.

As I make way,
as I make space,
as I make energy,
as I make love

to encompass
all that I am,
all that I've
becum.

April 30, 2022

Chapters Past

Snow-capped peaks,
blaring blue skies.
When I saw them
take the stage
my eyes tried to cry.

A bookstore filled with gems,
black cats at my feet,
a warm hug to greet,
incense and oils fill
the room ripe with healing.

Friends of olden days,
places keyed by frays
of a life once lived
in this city once lit
with my own flames.

A chapter of carving
new space for the garments
of lessons and learnings,
pain broken freshly open
and shadows brought to light.

Congratulations, she said,
quite a ways you've come,
such an integral journey
of coming undone
to piece together perfectly

into a scene as divine
as the blue and pink sunset
painting over the snowy tops
with new paths carved
by the water melting downwards.

Filling streams of futures
unwritten but willing
to inhale a deep fresh breath
of air untainted
by a chapter long ago.

Dear Reader

Thank you for sharing this beautiful and gut-wrenchingly painful journey with me. This poetry has poured out of me during my journey of coming to know and befriend death. If I leave you with nothing else, I beckon you to remember this:

Death is not to be feared. Death is beautiful in its own right, and it is quite literally everywhere around you. Suffering and pain are natural experiences of life. And it is only when we fully embrace, commune and dance with our suffering that we open to receive more joy. Joy does not exist without suffering.

So, I urge you, rather than suppressing it, pushing it away, pretending it's not there–face it. Name it, see it, touch it, appreciate, and hold it. Your pain will teach you, will help you to expand, and will carve out an opening inside of you to fill to the brim with ecstatic bliss. And you are worthy of that. We are all worthy of this expression of love because quite simply, we are made of love.

May you continue to die again and again. For it is only through death that we come to know rebirth.

Thank you for witnessing my surrendering. I, with both intention and humility, summon yours through the sharing of this powerful and freeing work.

Blessed be, blessed be, blessed be.

Hunni Bloom

ACKNOWLEDGMENT

I want to give a heartfelt shoutout to my psychologist, Karen Trevithick (she's licensed in both Colorado and Illinois, y'all!). I believe healing happens through many, many different modalities.

And one size most certainly does not fit all. But for me, talk therapy has been one of my primary ways and spaces to heal within. I've worked with Karen for several years, and she bared witness to grief and processing around Tabby's death. On more times than I could ever count, Karen has held healing and transformative space for me as I've worked through my own tribulations.

I want to also express gratitude to my mother, Ruth. Mama, you've always been my number 1 fan. I know it was difficult for you to read and learn of many of the things expressed throughout my poetry. But nonetheless, you've stood by me, as you always do. I am my mother's daughter, and I wouldn't have it any other way.

Finally, though he will never read this, I want to pay tribute to my new soul-mate pet, Moon. My partner, Ryan, and I got Moon only a few short weeks after Tabby's passing. We were on our way home from a trip to California to see the Red Woods when I told Ryan as we sat in the San Francisco airport that I wanted us to get a cat. I knew I was nowhere near ready for another dog yet, but I had too much love to express and needed an animal in our home to receive it. "I want to get a boy cat, that's black with white spots, because I want him to be the opposite of Tabby," I told Ryan. He shook his head in agreement. "And I want to name him Moon," I declared. Ryan has an incredible way of never doubting me. "Okay, we will find Moon then," he told me. Moments later I pulled our local animal shelter website up on my phone and there he was–a boy, black with white spots, kitten named 'Moon Moon.' And that was that. He's been an integral part of my healing journey (and quite a few poems throughout this collection are about him!). Thanks for your unconditional love, Moon!

About Hunni Bloom

She is a poet and writer for the self-healers and change-makers.

Hunni Bloom was born in the sunshine state, came of age in the ancient Appalachian mountainside, dared to dream in the magnificent Rocky Mountains, then found her roots and created her home-place in the expansive heartland. She is currently home in Arcola, Illinois.

She has a Ph.D. in words (communication), is a military Veteran and is a certified yoga instructor. Hunni Bloom is in love with the moon, knows a woman's power lies within her sexual and creative energy, ritually communes with nature, and wholeheartedly believes everyone can fly.

@hunni_bloom

www.ingramcontent.com/pod-product-compliance
Lightning Source LLC
LaVergne TN
LVHW051728080426
835511LV00018B/2943
9798985311938